BE QUIET!

Written by Dina Anastasio ■ Illustrated by Jean Pidgeon

MODERN CURRICULUM PRESS

PROJECT DIRECTOR: Susan Cornell Poskanzer   PRODUCT MANAGERS: Christine A. McArtor
                          Leslie A. Baranowski   Denise Smith
EXECUTIVE EDITOR: Wendy Whitnah
ART DIRECTOR: Lisa Olsson
DESIGNER: Menny Borovski

Published by Modern Curriculum Press

MODERN CURRICULUM PRESS
13900 Prospect Road, Cleveland, Ohio 44136

A Paramount Communications Company

This edition is published simultaneously in Canada by
Globe/Modern Curriculum Press, Toronto.

ISBN 0-8136-1337-X (STY PK)   ISBN 0-8136-1338-8 (BB)   ISBN 0-8136-1339-6 (SB)

4 5 6 7 8 9 10   98

The queen was sleeping in her room.

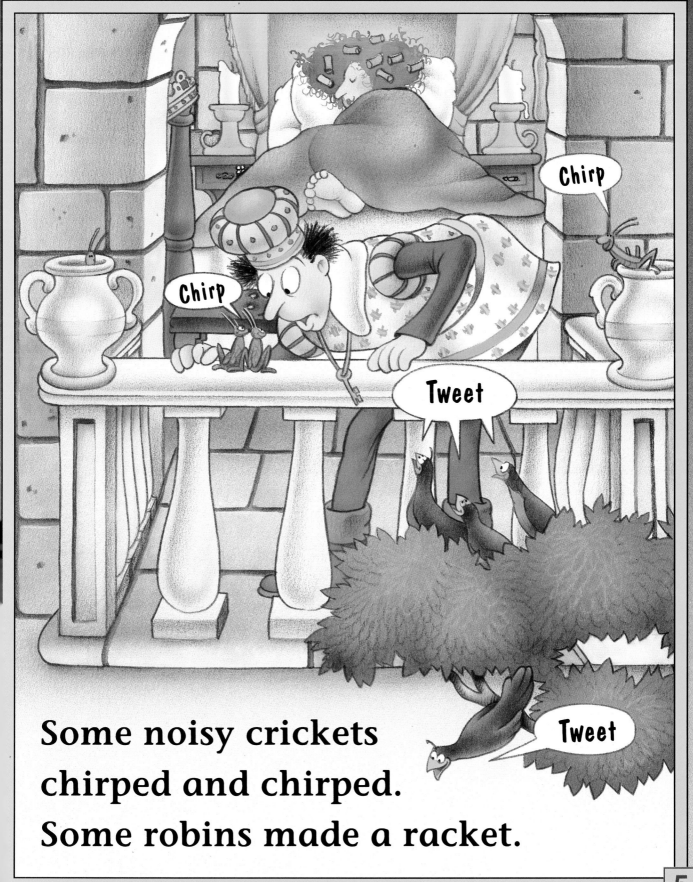

Some noisy crickets
chirped and chirped.
Some robins made a racket.

A duck stopped by. It quacked and quacked.

Two frogs appeared.
They croaked and croaked.
They really made a racket.

"Be quiet!" roared Sir Hackett.

"The queen must really have her rest.
You cannot make this racket!"

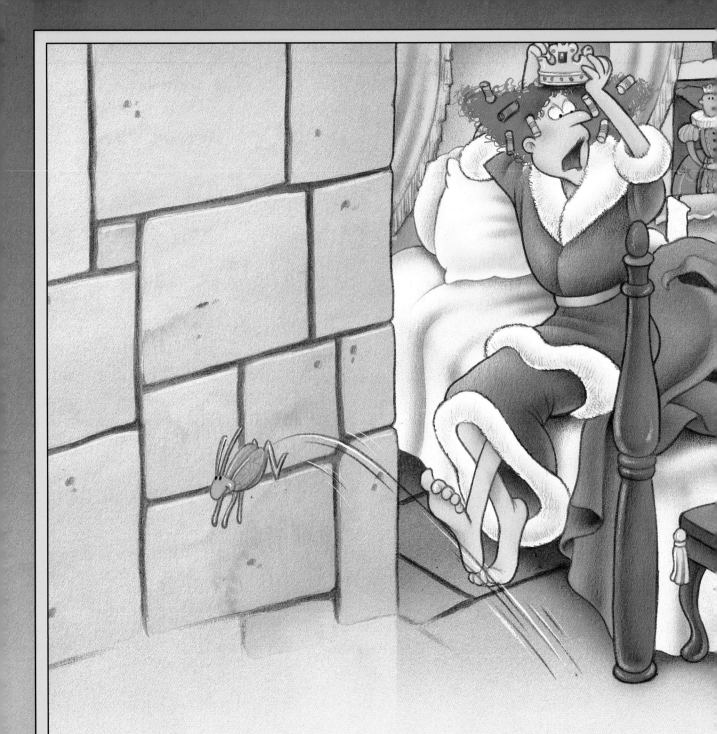

"You woke me up!" roared the queen.
"Be quiet, please, Sir Hackett.

I would have slept the night away.

But **you** made such a racket!"